I Spy

by Lorraine Sintetos
illustrations by Gary Undercuffler

Harcourt Brace & Company
Orlando Atlanta Austin Boston San Francisco Chicago Dallas New York Toronto London

"Hi, Clyde!" said Di.
"Let's play."
"Hi, Di!" said Clyde.
"Let's play I SPY."

"Why not?" said Di. "I'll try!"
"Fine," said Clyde. "What do you spy, Di?"

"I spy something in the sky," said Di. "It flies with no wings."

"You spy a kite!" cried Clyde.
"You're sly, Clyde," said Di.
"What do *you* spy?"

"I spy something that flies, too," said Clyde. "But it's not in the sky."

"Hmmm," said Di. "What do you have in mind?"

"Give up?" cried Clyde.

"Yes," said Di. "What flies but isn't in the sky?"

"Time!" cried Clyde.
"Time flies!"
"Clyde," said Di,
"you're so smart."
"What do you spy, Di?"
asked Clyde.

"I spy a fry," said Di. "I spy a fry that cries."

"Well," said Clyde, "what kind of fry can cry?"

"It's small," said Di.
"A small fry that cries?" said Clyde. "I give up!"

"It's a child!" cried Di. "A child is a small fry. And that child is crying!"

"Di, you're sly!" said Clyde.

"Time is flying by," said Di.
"I have to go. Bye, Clyde."
"Good-bye, Di," said Clyde.
"Let's play I SPY next time!"